LISTENING

Norman Wakefield

LISTENING

A Christian's
Guide to
Loving Relationships

WORD BOOKS
PUBLISHER
WACO, TEXAS

in gratitude

Many people have contributed to this book through what they have added to my life. I have expressed in writing what others have impressed on me.

This book is dedicated to some of the special people in my life:

—Dot and Wilfred Townsend, my mother- and father-in-law. They have always encouraged me to invest in eternal values. Their friendship and support are priceless.

—My church family, Shared Life Fellowship. I trust that I have been a good listener to these my brothers and sisters in Christ. They are special friends, encouragers, and ministers to me.

contents

one

LISTENING
IS A MINISTRY

YOU HAVE RECENTLY been thrust into a position of national leadership. For some time you've known it was coming. Your father held the position prior to you. He often reminded you that someday you would carry the nation's welfare on your shoulders. He prepared you for the task as fully as possible.

The appointment had hardly been made when you were confronted with difficult decisions. How do you unify the nation now that your father has died? What action will best cope with dissenters who already have attempted to usurp your authority? The weight of leadership rests heavily on your shoulders.

God is a special source of strength to you. *Why not turn to him for support,* you think. Thus, you plan a brief retreat to a small community nearby. You go there often when you need spiritual renewal—a few days alone to meditate, think, and worship.

The trip to the retreat center heightens your anticipation. Something inside tells you that this was a wise decision. As familiar friends greet you at the center, a sense of God's presence surrounds you.

Prayer. How you've looked forward to time alone, hidden away with God. How good it is to leave the business of the government at the capital. Now it's just the two of you. Time for refreshment, worship, renewal.

One evening you stretch out on your bed to relax. The sense of personal peace and physical comfort overcomes you and you fall asleep. You dream. Or is it a dream? God appears in his awesome splendor. The sense of his presence makes you tremble.

He speaks.

"Ask for whatever you want me to give to you."

You weren't prepared for that. *I can ask my Sovereign Lord for whatever I want!* Many thoughts begin to flash through your mind. The greatest kingdom on earth. Riches beyond measure; gold, silver, and precious jewels. Power to control men, yes, even to do miracles. Long life with perfect health.

Though these visions vie for center stage, another thought seeks to capture your attention. What is it that wants to be heard? Wisdom to be an effective leader of your nation. Wisdom? *But I already have a good mind. Why, before Dad died he affirmed that I am a man of wisdom. And in these early months of ruling I've demonstrated that I have what it takes.*

Still . . . it requires such discernment when people come to me with complex issues. Even with the keen mind and insight I possess I often feel the pressure of the decisions I must make. I do want so badly to be a godly leader.

"All right, my Lord, here it is. You've placed me in this awesome and demanding position of national leadership. I'm only a young man—sometimes I feel like a child. More and more I realize I don't know enough to fulfill my duties successfully. The decisions I'm called on to make overwhelm me at times. I feel the crushing responsibility for this nation of people. So here's my request: give your servant a listening heart to provide wise, effective leadership. Yes, a *listening heart.* I want the supernatural capacity to hear with the heart, to be able to separate right from wrong, to be able to make wise, accurate decisions. After all, how else can I adequately lead such a great nation as this? That's my request, dear Lord—give me supernatural listening ability to hear from the heart."

The Lord smiles. He is pleased. He is glad you've chosen something infinitely more priceless than long life, wealth, or international supremacy. He speaks, "I will grant what you have asked. I will give you a wise and listening heart. There has never been nor will there ever be a person as competent to hear with the inner ear. Listen with this inner ear and you will be a wise and just leader."

You awaken.

Did you recognize the incident I've just described? It is drawn from the biblical account of King Solomon's early years as king of Israel. Did you realize that Solomon's famous request was to be a skilled *listener?* To hear with the inner ear? Most translations use the words *understanding* or *discerning,* but the Hebrew word literally means "hearing." Solomon recognized that to be an effective leader he needed to be an effective listener.

This is very significant to me. It highlights how crucially important listening ability is to effective interpersonal relations. Every day we are bombarded with messages of varying degrees of significance. As we grow up we decide what to listen to and what to filter out. Sometimes we interpret what we hear to bring it into harmony with our personal life view. Our listening skills—or the lack of them—affect us profoundly!

God Listens

The story of Solomon demonstrates an essential part of God's nature. God listens. He is always in touch with his entire creation, and he is able to communicate not only with the works of his hand, but also with his responding creation.

Let's make it more personal—God listens to you. Ponder that a moment. Isn't it incredible! The sovereign Lord of the universe *listens* to you and to me. What a practical expression of his amazing grace!

I know that this is true because the Scriptures specifically record it. Our Lord *hears* children crying.

Abraham had sent Hagar, Sarah's servant, away with her child Ishmael. They wandered in the desert until their water and food were exhausted. In this pitiful condition mother and son began to weep in despair. Notice what the Scripture says:

> God heard the boy crying, and the angel of God called to Hagar from heaven and said to her, "What is the matter, Hagar? Do not be afraid; God has heard the boy crying as he lies there. Lift the boy up and take him by the hand, for I will make him into a great nation" (Gen. 21:17, 18).

God's hearing is so sensitive that he is attuned to the cries of young children. He wants to listen to the sobs and laughter of the youngest. I find this a profound thought that challenges me as a parent and teacher. If God takes time to listen to children, I too want to listen.

God listens to his older family members—you and me. He heard the Israelites as they groaned under the inhuman Egyptian bondage. "The Israelites groaned in their slavery and cried out. . . . God heard their groaning" (Exod. 2:23, 24). The heart of the God of kindness and mercy must have been deeply touched as he listened to his children weep in agony under the crushing load of tyranny. He listened.

The psalmist repeatedly acknowledges that the Lord heard him as he cried out. David's distress is evident in Psalm 6. He uses phrases such as "my bones are in agony" (v. 2), "my soul is in anguish" (v. 3), "I am worn out from groaning; all night long I flood my bed with weeping and drench my couch with tears" (v. 6). In verses 8 and 9 he declares his confidence that "the Lord has heard my weeping. The Lord has heard my cry for mercy." God listens.

God's compassionate, listening heart is seen clearly in Jesus Christ. During his earthly visit he attracted multitudes, not merely by what he said, but equally by his willingness to listen to the individual's distressing circumstances. After hearing the full message, he would respond with the appropriate word or touch. Jesus listens.

Jesus also expresses the full meaning of listening. Because he could hear the full message, he could always respond appropriately. Frequently we meet people who do not listen effectively and who thus respond incorrectly or not at all. Not so with God. His response is always appropriate because he knows what the whole issue or situation is.

Christ affirmed the Father as a listening God. As he stood before Lazarus's tomb he cried out to the Father, "Father, I thank you that you have heard me. I knew that you always hear me" (John 11:41, 42). In this delightful affirmation we can know that we, too, always have access to the ear of our heavenly Father. He is the listening God.

So what's the point? You say, "I've always known that God can hear. What's so special about that?" I find three implications from the fact that God is a listening God. First, God chooses to listen to his creation—especially man. How thankful I am that God did not create man and then leave him to fend for himself. Instead, God is vitally involved in our lives, actively communicating with us.

Second, the fact that God listens tells me that he recognizes man's basic need for a listener. All of us cry out to be listened to. God knew we would have that need; it appears to be basic to our nature. We were not created to live in isolation.

Third, God dignifies the act of listening. He makes it a ministry. In our relationship with both Christians and non-Christians we have the happy privilege of exemplifying this exciting aspect of our Father's nature—that he cares enough to listen. Every act of listening has the potential of being a ministry of the Spirit of God. Every time I listen I reflect the likeness of the listening Father.

Three Ways Listening Can Change Your Life

Like Solomon, you can become a discerning, sensitive, listener. You can learn to listen using both mind and heart. And your choice to grow in this area of life has at least three significant implications for you:

1) *Perceptive listening will make you wiser.* I started this chapter relating Solomon's plea for a deeper capacity to listen perceptively. We know the outcome of that request—Solomon became famous for his wisdom. Later he was to record, "Let the wise listen and add to their learning" (Prov. 1:5). He spoke about the blessing that comes to the person who listens for wisdom, "watching daily at my doors" (Prov. 8:34).

Perceptive listening enlarges one's sphere of input. It represents an active receiving process which makes more information and insight available to the listener. An active, perceptive listener is more in touch with his environment, with people, events, and things. The first person to benefit from listening is the listener himself.

2) *Perceptive listening will help you build stronger interpersonal rela-*

tionships. People tend to seek out the perceptive listener. This is especially true of the listener who demonstrates empathy for the speaker—or for the listener who is willing to actively help the person with a problem.

For a number of years I asked individuals to describe the person who had most influenced his or her life. I discovered that a consistent pattern of characteristics emerged and that one recurring feature was listening. A person who influences another's life expresses interest in that person and demonstrates a desire to hear about his ideas, activities, problems, and so on. By listening he expresses his wish to have a two-way relationship.

Through the act of listening, we frequently pick up clues that someone else is seeking a relationship with us. I recall speaking at a conference some time ago on the subject of building interpersonal relationships. One of the participants, a teenager, decided to practice on her dad one of the concepts I'd proposed. She went to him and expressed a desire for them to go out for lunch together. He made some excuse, so she tried another tactic. Still he did not pick up the clues. Finally, later in the day, his wife said to him, "Your daughter wants to work on her relationship with you. She's been trying to get a lunch date with you."

Later, the girl's father related this incident to me and commented on how much he needed to work on his listening skills so that he would not miss other opportunities. Daily, people are seeking out individuals with whom they can relate. Listening skills are among our most important resources in furthering the relational process.

3) *Perceptive listening will increase the impact of your personal ministry.* One of my goals in writing this book is to get Christians excited about the potential of developing their listening ability. Many people pay high fees to seek the expertise of listening specialists; we call these specialists counselors,

psychologists, or psychiatrists. I am enthusiastic about helping nonspecialists increase their listening skills, because I know the power of effective listening. I am certain it is a very significant form of ministry available to anyone who would like to develop it.

Let me suggest five reasons perceptive listening is a valuable ministry to others:

One, perceptive listening helps others express their *feelings* in a constructive manner. When an individual is frustrated, angry, discouraged, or frightened, he usually looks for some means to express it. The listener helps him talk out the emotions, feeding back what he hears to help the process of sorting and clarification. Through this ventilation process, the emotions are discharged constructively, and the troubled person is able to turn to healthy solutions.

Two, perceptive listening helps others talk out ideas, problems, and decisions which need resolving. We all are faced almost constantly with new information or decisions which we need to think through. Many times the simple act of talking out whatever is confronting us helps us sort out information, opinions, and conflicts. I have discovered that this is a helpful process when I am preparing a sermon, planning to write a book, facing a significant decision, or clarifying some information that is unclear to me.

Three, empathetic listening is one of the best means of expressing unselfish love. Listening says, "You are important," or "Your ideas, problems, and feelings are important to me. I care about you." Listening is a primary means of modeling God's love. Think of that! What a potential for Christ's people to relate to one another in a practical way. We show others we love them by the way we listen to them.

That's true for me. When I have something I feel the need to share, I deeply appreciate someone who will listen intently, expressing loving care. By contrast, I'm frustrated by the individual who constantly interrupts, changes the subject, or seems disinterested—especially when I'm discouraged or excited and want so much to share my experience. Thank God, *He* always listens.

Four, perceptive listening provides the foundation for wise counsel. James reminds us that we are to "be quick to listen, slow to speak and slow to become angry" (James 1:19). Only by listening patiently and perceptively can we prepare ourselves to understand another's struggle adequately and to respond in a helping way. Quick advice frequently speaks to a false problem.

One reason I'm sold on the ministry of listening is this: I've discovered that careful listening is often essential to finding the real source of the problem. Frequently what a person *thinks* is his problem or need is not the real one at all, but only the felt or perceived one. As he talks it out with a perceptive listener, he begins to see other dimensions of which he was unaware, and which greatly influence the solution.

Five, listening says, "I want to understand you. I want to know you." It is one of the most basic ways to convey a sense of respect, to treat another with dignity. Through this act we affirm to another person that God is willing to listen, that he eagerly waits for his troubled child to come to him and discover the compassion and deep concern of his loving Father.

Unquestionably, the listening I have been speaking about is a powerful form of ministry. Such listening embodies something of the nature of God himself. It makes available to the Holy Spirit a channel through which to communicate love and a helpful, appropriate response. This ministry is available to any one of God's family who longs to be available to his fellow family members.

Time to Reflect

The following response guide will help you evaluate your listenability. After completing the evaluation, consider asking a family member or close friend to share his or her perspective on the kind of listener you are. Choose someone who will give you honest feedback.

---

1. Fill out the following chart by checking the appropriate response to each statement.

I consider listening a very important way to minister to another person.	☐ *never* ☐ *sometimes* ☐ *usually*
Others would say that I am "slow to speak, and quick to hear."	☐ *never* ☐ *sometimes* ☐ *usually*
I can decide what I should listen for when someone comes to talk to me.	☐ *never* ☐ *sometimes* ☐ *usually*
I can identify situations in which I am a poor listener. I know how to cope with them.	☐ *never* ☐ *sometimes* ☐ *usually*
When others are speaking, my mind wanders.	☐ *never* ☐ *sometimes* ☐ *usually*

When I disagree with someone I "shut them out" of my listening.	□ *never* □ *sometimes* □ *usually*
I interrupt others when they are speaking.	□ *never* □ *sometimes* □ *usually*

2. Complete the following statements:
   a. My listening would be a greater ministry if I _____
   _____.

   b. Two people who would say that I am a sensitive listener are _____ and _____.

two

OBSTACLES TO
EFFECTIVE LISTENING

My friend Rick Stapleton has a fascinating story to tell. Let's listen in as he relates it . . .

It all began on a Tuesday night when Jill, my wife, told me she had signed us up for a listening seminar the following weekend.

"A listening seminar! Who needs that?" I asked. "I hear fine."

Still we ended up going. Jill talked me into it. A mutual friend had spoken highly of it and encouraged us to go. So, we went!

The seminar leader began by citing research showing how inefficient many people are at listening. He stressed the difference between *hearing* and *listening.* According to him, hearing relates to the physical process by which we receive sounds in our brain, an automatic process that occurs without noticeable effort. Listening, by contrast, is *a skill one learns.* We learn to perceive or to ignore voices, music, noises—the sounds that surround us. We learn to "tune in" or "tune out."

Chet, one of the participants, told about a "Dennis the

Menace" cartoon he had seen. Dennis goes to Mr. Wilson, his neighbor, who is reading the newspaper, and gives him a warm, "Hello, Mr. Wilson." No response. Dennis speaks a little louder. "Hello, Mr. Wilson." Still no response. Finally, Dennis blasts forth with, "HELLO, MR. WILSON!" No answer. Dennis turns to leave and in a normal voice says, "Well, then, goodbye, Mr. Wilson." Mr. Wilson replies, "Goodbye, Dennis." As he walks out the door Dennis remarks, "There's nothing wrong with his hearing, but his listening's not so good."

We had a good laugh, but I felt a bit uncomfortable as I recalled my experience the night before. Danny, my seven-year-old, had wanted to talk to me but I had ignored him because I wanted to finish the newspaper. This seminar was getting too personal!

The leader then raised an important question, "When are you a poor listener?" He pointed out that certain conditions, situations, or attitudes might influence our listenability. All of us were silent as we pondered this question.

Alicia, an attractive young lady, broke the silence. "When I'm defensive I don't listen well. Yesterday Burt brought up a problem we've not resolved, and I could feel my barriers go up. I began to think up all the reasons he was wrong and I was right. Because the situation is very current, I'm aware that I was not listening thoughtfully to what my husband was trying to say."

Alicia's comment generated considerable discussion. I learned that *defensiveness* is a fairly common problem in family arguments. These situations are "duelogues" rather than "dialogues." Each person is busy thinking up an effective remark to "shoot down" the other's comments. Since we are not listening perceptively, we miss some of the most important information and emotions the other person is trying to express.

Someone pointed out that defensiveness may not reveal itself outwardly. The individual may resort to meek agreement or silence. Inside, however, he carries on his personal conversation, denying what the speaker is saying, justifying his own course of action as proper, shifting the blame to someone else, and so on. During this process, the bulk of his mental energy is consumed in nonlistening activities.

The leader observed that we *learn* to be defensive. Consequently, we can learn a more helpful form of relating. We can become more sensitive to situations in which we habitually raise our defenses, and we can practice more profitable listening habits.

I knew I needed to think more about my own defensiveness.

Cam, a distinguished-looking man with graying hair, moved us to a second issue. "I'm a talker. Maybe it's some ego need I have—I don't know. But I do know that I get more satisfaction from talking than from listening. If I have to sit quietly too long in a discussion, I can hardly contain myself. I feel the urge to express my opinions.

"Carole and I have discussed how this influences our relationship. We both agree that I tend to be less sensitive to her needs. I'm too impatient and end up butting in, interrupting her. Then she doesn't want to continue the conversation." With a laugh Cam added, "We've agreed I need to memorize that part of James 1:19 which says 'be quick to listen, slow to speak!' "

I think those of us who are like Cam don't realize the great value of listening. We need to see what a ministry of love it is to encourage others to speak, then to involve ourselves in listening intently, becoming genuinely interested in what the other person is sharing.

It also occurred to me that interrupting, like defensiveness, is a habit we learn. It may be stimulated by our impatience with others. In dealing with this obstacle we may need not only to work on breaking the habit but also to allow God to help us become more relaxed and patient.

Roy, a portly fellow who spoke very enthusiastically,

opened up a third area for us to consider. "My wife, Marcia, has helped me see that I often overload people with too much information. When I talk, I may speak for three or four minutes solid. Marcia has helped me realize that I dump too much information on a person at one time; it's too much to digest. Now I'm working at speaking for shorter periods of time."

Two thoughts immediately surfaced in my own mind. One, Roy was identifying a *speaker* problem which hinders effective listening. The first two had been primarily listener problems. I can see that the speaker, too, can create situations or obstacles that hinder perceptive listening.

The second thought carried me back to my job environment. A couple of days ago I was in my office with two fellow workers. One fellow was enthusiastic about a new idea he had. He spoke continuously for fifteen minutes. During that time I needed to ask questions but he gave me no opportunity. When he was finally finished I was aware that I felt extremely weary from having listened continuously for such a long period to so much information.

Roy gave a clue to resolve the problem. He said, "I am learning to speak for shorter periods of time. By breaking five minutes of monologue into one-minute units I give my listener an opportunity to "digest" what I've said. If something needs clarifying he can ask a question. If he wants to express his opinion or give additional information he can. What I like best about speaking in shorter units of time is that it helps keep my listener involved. He not only listens, but responds."

We were ready to move on to discover another situation in which we tend to be poor listeners. Patty's insight helped us this time. She said, "I don't listen well when I have other pressing things on my mind. My mind keeps moving back and forth and I become confused."

Nikki's eyes lit up as she spoke. "I can identify with

that. Yesterday a friend phoned to share a difficult problem she was experiencing. I had just put meat in the pressure cooker and I needed to watch the time. Then in comes Marty, our seven-year-old, to tell me about the problem he's having with his sister. I felt like I was playing ping pong, tossing horse shoes, and skiing all at the same time! Finally, out of desperation, I told my friend I'd call her back after supper so we could talk further."

Every participant in the seminar seemed to identify with this problem. Our leader helped us see that two separate problems may actually be involved. He spoke first of *internal* distractions or concerns which hinder effective listening. Though nothing in the room distracts me, things in my mind do: I'm worried about whether my son got back to college safely; I keep thinking about a disturbing remark my husband made as he left for work; I'm bothered that I'm not prepared for the test I have tomorrow. It's difficult to listen because I'm conscious of all the work I must accomplish today.

Our leader suggested a way to cope with these internal concerns—to resolve the internal concern before we proceed with the conversation. I may say, "I'd like to continue listening, but I'm so pressured with a work deadline that I can't concentrate well on our conversation. Could we talk further this evening?" Or, we may discipline our minds to lay aside the competing problem and focus on an immediate concern.

The second problem relates to *external* distractions or competing speakers. The seminar leader asked us to envision a situation: "Imagine that your favorite team is in the championship play-offs; it's the final game, and it's being televised. In fact, you're watching it right now. The doorbell rings. In come your brother and sister-in-law, who are passing through town and only have three hours to visit with you. You turn the TV down so you can talk *and* watch—right? Now you're trying to listen to both the game and your brother. It will likely be frustrating for both of you. Yet you're unwilling to give up either one."

As we discussed this listening problem, we agreed that those who need to be heard can help the listener by choosing the appropriate time to discuss personal matters—not when the listener is motivated to listen to someone or something else. Sometimes we accuse others of being poor listeners when we have approached them at unsuitable times.

Carole opened up a fifth issue that hindered perceptive listening. She said, "Cam and I discovered that we often try to discuss important issues at the wrong time. I'm thinking particularly of when I am *too tired* to listen well. Physical fatigue makes listening a chore. We found that bedtime was not the best time for heavy conversation. I ended up fighting to stay awake and Cam would become frustrated or angry. Then I felt guilty because I couldn't listen to what he wanted to share. Thankfully, we've resolved this by setting aside time to talk when we're rested and alert."

During this discussion we came to see that mental as well as physical fatigue dulled our listenability. Many of the twentieth-century vocations tax mental energy as much or more than physical energy. When husband and/or wife comes home from work, they may want to escape serious conversation which demands careful listening.

I recalled numerous incidents when I had returned home from exhausting mental work to be greeted by a lovely wife and five excited children who wanted to update me on their day's activities. I had learned to be honest with them, telling them when I needed fifteen minutes to relax before relating.

As I pondered all that had been said, I discovered one more listening obstacle I'd struggled with. Turning to my group members I said, "I confess to another listening barrier! In reflecting on our discussion I see that I've erected listening barriers *toward certain individuals.* I can think of a person I work with whom I regularly turn off. Just the tone of her voice sends me into orbit. Also, her constant complaining irritates me. I find her a very difficult person to listen to."

The other group members nodded their heads, and I knew that they could identify with what I was describing. I recalled a friend of mine saying that for years he had felt that women had little of significance to say. He had never listened to them with the same intensity, the same level of anticipation as he had to men. Fortunately, in the past couple of years he had discovered that women have minds as keen as those of men. This recognition had revolutionized his appreciation of, and relationship to, women. But for years before that my friend's bias had influenced his listenability toward women.

We can hold biased attitudes toward the opposite sex, different age groups ("teenagers are ding-a-lings; they don't know much"), ethnic minorities, certain personality types, and so on. Failing to listen seriously to members of these groups is one specific way we express these attitudes.

After summarizing what we had discovered, our seminar leader dismissed us for the evening. As my wife and I walked back to our room, I summarized again in my mind the obstacles we had explored: defensiveness, urge to talk, information overload, internal and external pressures, poor timing, physical and mental fatigue, and negative attitudes. I decided that I needed to develop an approach to coping with obstacles to listening. I wanted to be a perceptive listener. Thus, in the days ahead I came up with the following plan.

Five Ways to Remove Listening Obstacles

1) *Identify the obstacle.* What is (are) the specific obstacle (or obstacles) that hinders my listenability? Of the seven

mentioned in this chapter, which limits me most? That will be the one on which I want to focus my energy first.

It is also helpful to identify the person or persons who are most affected by the obstacle. Does my defensiveness hinder my communication most when I am talking with my spouse? By identifying the person, I become more aware of the relationship that needs the most attention.

2) *Identify who controls the obstacle.* If I am defensive, then *I* control the obstacle because it is within me (though another's comments may encourage or discourage defensiveness). One with the "urge to talk" controls the obstacle more than the listener does. Poor timing is more likely to be a problem controlled both by the listener and the one who wants to talk.

Identifying who controls the obstacle is important because it helps us see whether the problem is ours or another person's problem which affects us. Once this is realized, the people involved may need to work together to *rearrange the conditions,* in order to develop a more satisfying communication process. Rearranging the conditions may involve any strategy which will remove the obstacle: working on defensiveness, finding a better place to talk, applying a specific communication principle, and so on.

3) *Determine level of commitment.* Do I want to change my present behavior or attitudes? How important is it to me to change present defeating patterns? What will it cost? Am I ready to expend the energy necessary to work for personal growth daily?

4) *Develop sensitivity to defeating situations.* When am I usually physically fatigued? Toward whom do I hold unhealthy attitudes? What internal pressures typically erode my listenability?

This step acquaints me with the facts and circumstances related to my listening obstacle. If I come to see that Thursday night is typically a difficult time because my husband wants to talk but I am always worn out, then I know I want to focus my energy on changing the Thursday night defeat pattern.

5) *Work out a practical plan.* What would be one practical step to change the situation? In the illustration above it might be to (a) take an afternoon nap, (b) schedule supper later so we can talk when he gets home, (c) go out for supper to a quiet relaxing environment, (d) agree to talk after supper and after we've both had an hour to relax.

Usually, there is some practical step I can take to begin to move from obstacle to opportunity. Will I commit myself to work on the solution?

Removing Listening Obstacles

Rick's story contains a lot of helpful information about how listening obstacles can hinder effective communication—and how they can be overcome. The following exercises are designed to help you apply the principles Rick learned and to help you remove your own listening obstacles. In working through the exercises, try to be as practical as possible. Work out solutions, and determine which obstacle is most important to tackle *this* week.

---

1. Fill in the chart on the following page as completely as possible, based on your own experience. Which is the biggest problem to you in your own listening situations?

2. Think through the following habit patterns. Which ones do you think you have learned? Choose one to concentrate on changing.

Obstacle to Effective Listening	Toward whom?	Recent Example	Practical Steps toward Solution
Defensiveness			
Urge to talk			
Information overload			
Internal/external pressures			
Poor timing			
Physical/mental fatigue			
Negative attitude			

a. Ignoring others when reading newspaper or watching TV.
b. Trying to listen to someone when distracted by another interest.
c. Asking a family member to listen when he or she is weary, busy, or upset.
d. Talking for too long a time without allowing the listener to react.
e. Interrupting others while they are talking.
f. Becoming defensive when others tell me about my problems or weaknesses.
g. Falling asleep in church or Sunday school.
h. Other: _____

3. As a family, list topics that need to be discussed as a group or among individuals. Then decide on a time when these can be pursued with earnest attention.

three

LISTENING
FOR FEELINGS

The following test was given to 3001 graduate students at Egghead University. I'd like you to try to match wits with these learned persons. Later I'll tell you how they fared.

Read each of the following statements one at a time. After reading it, jot down how you would typically respond if someone would make that comment to you. What would you be likely to say?

> *Situation #1:* "I'm tired of this dumb homework. That stupid Mr. Barlow is always loading us with too much."
>
> *Response:*

Situation #2: "What's the use? I try and try but I never do it right. No wonder no one will hire me. I'm a loser."

Response:

Situation #3: "Leave me alone. You're always on her side. You think she's better than I am."

Response:

Situation #4: "Do you like me?"

Response:

Now that you've completed the test, I'll share how the E.U. students did. Of the 3001 who took the test, 2983 failed! The ingenius professor who designed the instrument found that his students were unsuccessful for two basic reasons. One, they didn't listen for the feelings being expressed and reflect them back to the speaker in an understanding manner. Two, they had a tendency to give advice—to moralize, command, criticize, or ridicule rather than really listen to what the speaker was trying to say. Responses like these usually are detrimental rather than helpful in the listening process.

Discovering a Vital Ministry

Conversation is the main vehicle for expressing feelings as well as ideas. And since feelings are continually looking for outlets, we can see that conversations are bound to be filled with feelings, some erupting and others edging their way out.[1]

In chapter one, I stated that perceptive listening is a significant form of ministry. I consistently find this true in my own life. Consider this example.

A few years ago our family moved from southern California to Phoenix, Arizona. During a househunting trip to Phoenix, Amy, our oldest daughter, expressed much criticism about the move. I recall one statement: "Why would anyone want to live in that stupid cowpatch town!" Winnie and I were baffled, because Amy is typically a cheerful, happy person. Finally, the problem surfaced during a conversation between mother and daughter. Amy was upset at the threat of leaving her friends behind, moving to a strange city, and entering a new school. As Winnie and I more fully identified with her feelings, we were able to be supportive and understanding. Listening was the key.

Let me suggest three reasons that listening for feelings is a powerful ministry. First, it is an *excellent means of showing empathy* for what someone else is experiencing. We are consistently touching the lives of people who are lonely, depressed, disappointed, shy, unloved, fearful, and frustrated. When we empathize with others, we try to identify with their feelings, conflicts, and emotions, and we try to relate to them in a caring manner. We may not necessarily agree with their behavior or lifestyle, but we "weep with those who weep" (Rom. 12:15, RSV). In order to empathize with others, however, we must determine just what they are feeling—and this requires perceptive listening.

As we listen for feelings, we frequently *help those to whom we listen get in touch with their own feelings*. This is a second

reason listening can be a ministry. Like a mirror, we can
reflect a person's feelings back to him in such a way that
he is able to understand more clearly what he is feeling.
It is not uncommon for someone to share his conflicts with
a good listener and in the process to discover feelings he
was not even aware of—feelings that were acting beneath
the surface.

A third reason listening ministers is that it *helps the speaker
ventilate emotions* that are causing problems. Talking out feelings of anger with a compassionate listener often helps re-
duce the intensity of that anger, and frees the speaker to
work on constructive solutions. Expressing fears to someone
who does not laugh, or preach, or glibly state that "Christians shouldn't fear" can enable someone who is struggling
to work through his fear to positive benefit.

Of course, talking out feelings is not a guarantee that
they will be resolved, but it is an early part of a problem-
solving process that can lead to positive results. Perceptive
listening can be of great help in that process.

Three Ways You Can Help

We as listeners can do much to help others deal with
their emotions. The attitudes we communicate, the way
we listen, our nonverbal communication—all these are being
observed by the speaker. He monitors us to see if it is
safe to speak honestly and express his inner emotions.

Here are some specific ways we can help:

1) *Encourage the speaker to express his or her feelings.* The idea
is to try to get him or her to elaborate on his feelings.
Then we want to listen without interrupting, or in any
other way hindering the expression of feelings. One reason
the "Typical Twelve" responses are not helpful is that by
their nature they discourage the flow of feelings. They do
not promote openness and release. They tend to imply,

"Don't feel that way"; "Don't say that"; or "You're bad to have those feelings."

2) *Put the other person in touch with his or her emotions.* Frequently a person cannot clearly identify the emotion that is frustrating or defeating him. We can help him identify the underlying feelings by giving him freedom to speak about them and by sharing what we hear him saying. Sometimes perceptive questions ("Did you feel angry after he did that?") are helpful. Remember, one of the special strengths of perceptive listening is that it puts the speaker more in touch with his feelings.

3) *Don't condemn feelings.* Emotions are a part of man's makeup. Sometimes they become difficult to control. Some emotions have been typed as "good" or "bad." Consequently, many people have developed a fear of expressing feelings.

Some people find it difficult to express *any* feelings. Others suppress certain feelings they perceive as unacceptable or inappropriate. The perceptive, caring listener attempts to give these individuals a secure environment in which to get in touch with these emotions and to talk them out.

Sadly we often create negative circumstances which inhibit true sharing. The troubled youth comes home to be criticized for feeling angry with his teacher. The wife wants someone with whom to share her feelings of insecurity, but her husband laughs about it. Will we ever realize the potential ministry of the listening ear?

Describing the Process

Perceptive listening for feelings and emotions is a two-step process that we must learn. And, like any skill, once it is learned it must be practiced until proficiency is gained.

Step one is *listening for feelings that underlie communication.* Sounds simple, doesn't it? In practice it is much more diffi-

cult. Yet, the point I have sought to make in this chapter
is that this is a most helpful ministry and worth mastering.
It pays rich dividends to the person in need.

Last night I sat down with a young lady in our church
family. During the conversation she related the intense
buildup of emotions that had been occurring during the
preceding week. Misunderstandings in interpersonal relations were creating tensions which erratically flared up. She
was in need of a listening ear and a compassionate heart.
Thus, for about forty-five minutes I listened and helped
my friend talk about the feelings being encountered and
then weigh possible courses of action.

At the conclusion of our discussion the familiar smile
had returned to my friend's face, and a renewed sense of
confidence in God's power to undertake had emerged.

Listening for feelings is difficult. One reason is that we
have many emotions which are not easily distinguished.
Is he feeling frustration or anger? Is it a feeling of superiority
or inner confidence? Does she feel trapped or fearful to
face old friends? Perhaps you have not realized the range
of emotions we experience.

Consider the following list:

Hurt	Inferior	Tense
Humiliated	Silly	Loved
Lonely	Jealous	Rejected
Intimidated	Sympathy	Disappointed
Hatred	Accepted	Frustrated
Hated	Protective	Impatient
Confident	Angry	Superior
Shy	Sad	Ashamed
Useless	Cheated	Trapped
Jubilant	Unworthy	Despair

Without practice and intense listening, few people can
effectively distinguish these emotions in conversations with
others. Most of us have not practiced the skill of differenti-

ating emotions enough to become proficient. Thus, our capacity to help others in this area is limited.

Another reason listening for feelings is difficult is that many people are not in touch with their feelings and cannot verbalize them. They may have grown up in homes where talking about or expressing feelings was not encouraged, and consequently never learned to be comfortable with their own emotions. Or they may have insulated themselves from their own emotions because of earlier experiences in which they were hurt.

I recall a young man who came for counseling. He had had three serious relationships with young women all of which had ended. By the time the first relationship terminated, he had developed strong feelings for the young lady. Her desire to end the relationship hurt him emotionally. When he met the second girl, he determined not to get as emotionally involved. Yet, as the relationship progressed, he found strong feelings growing toward the second girl. This relationship, too, was ended by the girl. By the time he was dating the third girl, he had carefully encapsulated his emotions to prevent himself from further hurt, and he expressed few feelings outwardly. Unfortunately, the third relationship ended because this young lady was seeking a man who could be more expressive of his feelings!

Listening for feelings is difficult for a third reason. Often the speaker "translates up." He translates his feelings into thought concepts or "hints." Rather than saying, "I'm fearful of your traveling forty miles per hour on this narrow winding road," a person may say, "I noticed the speed limit is twenty-five miles per hour." Or, rather than saying, "I'm lonely; would you stay home tonight?" he or she says, "I think you should stay home tonight."

I said that step one in the process of listening for feelings is trying to discern the emotions that underlie the communication. Step two is *reflecting the perceived feelings back to the speaker.* This step is as crucial as the first. It is the only way the

speaker knows if the listener is hearing the *full* communication, and whether the message has been received accurately.
Feeding back the perceived message to the speaker makes
it possible for him to acknowledge whether or not he has
been heard correctly.

Let's illustrate the process of reflecting back feelings by
looking at the beginning of this chapter. If my child says,
"I'm tired of this dumb homework. That stupid Mr. Barlow
is always loading us with too much," my response might
be, "You sound very frustrated with your homework and
angry at Mr. Barlow."

If I've heard correctly the feelings expressed and reflected
them back accurately, my child might respond, "Yeah, that's
right. That's how I feel." If not, then he can clarify the
feelings he has and I can check out my perceptions again.

Here's a second example you tried. A friend tells you:
"What's the use? I try and try but I never can do it. No
wonder no one will hire me. I'm a loser."

A helpful response might be, "I'm hearing you say that
you feel hopeless. You feel trapped by failure. Is that what
you're feeling?"

I know of no other area of communication which has
been more rewarding to me than the ministry of listening
for feelings. I still must discipline myself to practice this
skill—especially in family relationships. But whenever I do,
the results are gratifying. I feel that listening for feelings
is one of the essential elements of effective interpersonal
relationships. It is an integral element of ministry within
the Christian community.

Attitudes Influencing Outcome

As we develop the skill of listening for feelings, it is
essential that we cultivate the proper attitude. Skillful lis-

tening for feelings is much more meaningful when it is infused with a loving attitude. Let me describe several characteristics of the kind of attitude that can transform the process of listening for feelings into a vital ministry.

One is the desire to be helpful. We listen intently because we want to help another person get in touch with what is festering inside. We're genuinely interested in knowing what feeling our friend is trying to express. In a world which often communicates indifference and hatred, we want to communicate the love of God within us—and we show it by listening.

In addition, the best attitude is one of longing to hear the *full* communication. A careless listener usually will not hear clearly. The message of emotions is seldom easily heard. People usually don't scream, "I'm hurting!"; instead, they whisper it, in guarded statements, in test cases to see if the environment is safe. Consequently, the perceptive listener will have his senses trained to discern what is being said.

Two years ago my son, Joel, was involved in his school's wrestling program. One day he came home and announced, "Dad, I'm quitting the team." I was surprised, because I had received no earlier clues of his dissatisfaction. As Joel talked, I tried to practice the listening principles I've described in this chapter. After a while, Joel began to express frustration that the coach did not praise his efforts. We talked more. Then Joel revealed his fear of going to the center of the floor before his teammates and putting his wrestling skills on the line. I heard feelings of fear, defeat, and failure. Together, we talked through these feelings.

Joel finished the year on the wrestling team. He made the decision himself, but I'm confident that the experience of talking out his inner frustration and fear in a supportive environment was a large factor in his decision to continue. What impressed me most about this experience was the fact that the *real* problems were hidden until they were revealed and faced through the talking-listening process.

There is a third dimension of the listener's attitude that is essential. A helpful listener must provide an accepting, understanding environment in which the speaker can share his or her innermost feelings. Parents often lose excellent opportunities to support their children because they turn from understanding and acceptance to judgments, advice, threats, and so on. *This kind of attitude does not promote open, honest sharing.*

It is especially difficult to practice acceptance and understanding during those times when someone is expressing negative emotions about us or our behavior. A nondefensive posture on our part, however, will facilitate the expression of honest feelings and can lead to positive results.

I can think of two examples of this kind of situation in my own life. As a parent, I have found it difficult to be accepting and understanding when my children expressed feelings of injustice or disagreement with me. As a church leader, I have found it hard not to react defensively to church members who were not pleased with what I had done in my leadership capacity. In either of these situations, humbly listening to others as they expressed feelings against my actions was not easy. But I have found that such an attitude has been profitable for resolving the problem or conflict at hand.

Three Things Acceptance Does

The climate of acceptance is crucial because it accomplishes so much. First, it releases people from fear of judgment and opens them up to share honest feelings that have been troubling them. Many people are helped significantly through counseling when the counselor communicates an accepting, compassionate attitude. I have had people tell me that they have harbored defeating feelings for years but never experienced the accepting, nonjudgmental environment which freed them to share.

Second, acceptance creates a nondefensive environment. This is critical, because people typically throw up barriers to their innermost feelings if they think they are being attacked or judged. Do you? *Acceptance is not to be equated with agreement.* Acceptance says, "I accept your feelings as valid to you. I do not condemn you for having them."

Third, acceptance is a significant way to express the love of Christ. Through this compassionate spirit of understanding the individual is freed to explore the inner needs, conflicts, and goals of his life with a helping friend. He sees modeled in an earthly friend the loving concern of Christ.

This is important because our conceptions of God are shaped by the way others relate to us. Every so often I meet an individual who has developed a distorted view of God, and most of the time this distortion has come from faulty human models. An elderly lady once told me that she always felt God was stern and judgmental, that she could not feel from God the openness and acceptance she longed for. One of her parents had modeled this stern, judgmental attitude toward her, and the misconception she derived from her early experience had deeply influenced the way she had responded to God all her life. How much better to be living examples of the open love of Christ to those who need the kind of compassion he can provide!

Where Does Advice Come In?

Frequently during my workshops and seminars on listening someone will say, "You mean all I can do is listen when I know the person **is** doing something wrong?" To answer this question I stress that perceptive listening involves a sequence:

1. The speaker expresses the need to communicate emotion,
2. The listener practices perceptive, nonjudgmental listening,
3. The feeling is "talked out," and then
4. The listener shares his or her own perspective if needed or appropriate.

The sequence can be illustrated as follows:

need ——▶ listening ——▶ problem solving

It is important to remember the progression because the entire process can be short-circuited by a listener's tendency to advise, moralize, ridicule, or judge. Before solutions are discussed, the emotions must be adequately ventilated in an accepting climate. And I have found that, in the process, the speaker frequently works through his or her own constructive solutions without any "counsel." If I feel the need to share a biblical perspective or insight, I do it during the problem-solving segment which *follows* the feelings segment.

Developing the Skill

I have said that listening for feelings is not an easy skill to master. Therefore, as an exercise, I have provided a number of feeling statements to analyze. The fundamental question to answer about each is, "What feeling is the speaker expressing?" Use the list of emotions on page 40 to help you, but do not be limited to them.

When you have identified the feeling, jot down a response that reflects back to the speaker the feeling you think he is expressing. Remember, no *preaching, moralizing, advising, ridiculing.*

Statement	Feeling(s) being expressed	Appropriate response
"Teachers don't care! They load homework on us like we are slaves."		
"Guess what? We won! And I got the winning hit."		
"You like Tom better than me don't you?"		
"Couldn't you stay home tonight? I've been by myself every night this week."		
"I can't ask her for a date. She'd never go out with me."		

"I'm having a hard time studying the Bible but I'm going to master it somehow."		
"I made this all by myself; I think it's pretty."		
"I should not have done it. You had a right to be mad at me."		
"If he finds out, what'll I do? I've never been in trouble like this before."		
"Jim said I'd make sales if I did what he said. Today I sold three units. I think maybe I'll be able to do it."		
"I hate Sunday school. Mrs. Waters is the dullest teacher I've ever had. Why do you make me go?"		

four

LISTENING
FOR IDEAS

I AM A JOGGER. At this time of year in Phoenix, Arizona, where I live, the days are blistering hot. It is necessary for me to rise before the sun to run when it is cooler. I have come to prize the early morning when the city is still asleep and jogging is a quiet activity.

During those early morning runs, I often thank God for the abundant blessings he has given. I express appreciation for a healthy, coordinated body that functions smoothly. I thank him for energy to be productive through the day. And I express special gratitude for a mind that can be stimulated with new ideas, visions, and opportunities.

I have come to value my mind, my capacity to learn and explore life. And I have come to believe that one of the best ways a Christian can express gratitude to God for the gift of his mind is to develop it. Stupidity and intellectual laziness are not Christian virtues! In fact, the writer of Hebrews comments that individuals who "by constant use have trained themselves to distinguish good from evil" have the mark of maturity (Heb. 5:14). The words "constant use" are more literally translated "exercise." We train our minds, by exercising them, so that we can more carefully

49

distinguish between good and evil. What a foundation for wisdom!

I have found my own mind powerfully exercised and enriched through dialogue with others who also enjoy exercising their cognitive resources. In the exchange of ideas, concepts, and information, each person stimulates the other—if each is able to listen perceptively to what is being shared. Listening intently for ideas can bring us to new insight and awareness, introduce us to new facts, and lead us to see error or distortion in our present thoughts. Through careful, alert listening for ideas, we have the privilege of growing cognitively.

It is this kind of listening that is the subject of this chapter. By looking at some of the situations that can hinder our listenability, and by examining the skills that can enhance effective listening, we can train ourselves to become more alert and perceptive in processing the information and ideas we hear.

Who Owns the Problem?

As we listen for ideas, it is helpful to consider *why* we are listening—for what purpose and for whose benefit? We may be listening to help another person. For example, my daughter, Jill, may come to me and say, "Dad, I've got a problem I can't solve. Will you help me work on it?" So I listen carefully as she explains the issue she cannot resolve. I contribute my intellectual resources to help her think through the unresolved dilemma. I may be able to see some facet of the issue she does not see. Or, I may have additional information she does not have. As I listen intently, I enter into the problem with her and help her develop the resources to solve it.

Another reason we may listen for facts or ideas is to

solve a problem which two or more of us share. For instance, perhaps my wife, Winnie, and I face a common financial problem. She has some details which relate to a solution; I have other facts. Together we work to share our data so that our mutual problem can be resolved. Listening is essential. If I do not accurately hear the information she is sharing, we may not reach a satisfactory solution. If I receive the facts in a distorted manner, I may misinterpret what she says and we may end up in an argument.

Problems like the one above are common in the lives of most of us. Parent-child dilemmas, employee-employer disagreements, church leadership disputes—we could go on and on listing possibilities. Effective listening is an essential part of problem resolution in these situations.

Here's a third perspective. We listen for ideas because we ourselves have a problem or need. We require input from someone else, and we listen to receive the data that person possesses. For example, if I feel that my schedule is getting out of control, I may go to hear a lecture by a time-management expert. Or I may consult with a colleague about a personality conflict with which I am struggling.

There's another way of looking at this issue. In considering why we are listening for ideas in a particular situation, we are actually considering *who owns the problem*—another person who needs assistance, two or more of us who mutually share a problem, or we ourselves? Determining problem ownership in each situation helps us choose *how* to listen— what details to notice, what questions to ask, and so on.

Determining problem ownership can also alert us to barriers in our listening. It helps to ask ourselves, "How does the fact that she (or we, or I) owns the problem influence how I listen?" If we ourselves own the problem, for instance, we may find we are defensive and resist suggestions from other people.

A friend came to me recently to discuss a longstanding

personal problem. During the conversation he shared this example of how owning a problem can cause us to resist listening. "Norm," my friend said, "my wife shared several insights with me this week about my problem. I didn't want to hear them, but I recognized that she was right and *I must hear them.* I resolved to listen and it was most helpful."

There will always be times when we will have to "resolve to listen" to ideas. Understanding problem ownership can help us know when we are listening defensively.

Watch Out for Listening Filters!

The nature of the relationship between the speaker and the listener can be of great significance in the process of listening for ideas. A weak or injured relationship creates a situation in which *listening filters* are apt to be present. Listening filters are internal processes that cause a listener to leave out or change information, to inaccurately receive what is being communicated.

As you prepare to listen to another, ask yourself the following three questions. The answers will help you determine whether listening filters are present in the particular situation, and predict how these filters may distort the information the speaker is sharing:

Question 1: What is my attitude toward the speaker? Do I feel positive or negative toward him? Any of the following factors may influence how we feel about a given speaker:

Political persuasion	Social standing
Gender	Physical appearance
Race or nationality	Educational background
Religious convictions	Geographical location
Age	Lifestyle

Probably all of us are influenced by factors like these—often in ways we do not realize or want to acknowledge. I recall my first close encounter with black Christians. I had not been aware of any prejudice toward blacks until I was invited into their community and entered their homes. Suddenly I was confronted with unreasonable biases on my part of which I had been completely unaware. Until I resolved these biases, they threatened to influence my listenability toward members of this group.

Some listening filters are very subtle. Because someone uses a Bible translation others have criticized, do we tend to discredit all that the speaker is saying? Because she belongs to a "liberal" group do we close our ears? Or, once we've discovered that he's one of those "fundamentalists," do we decide he has nothing of significance to contribute?

Another subtle filter is the "lookalike" filter. If the speaker reminds us of a neighbor we couldn't tolerate, we may find ourselves disinterested in the speaker. Unfortunately, this may happen subconsciously; we may not realize that the basis for our not listening is very unsound.

Question 2: Who has conditioned me? Often we have been conditioned for or against the speaker by what others have said: "I hope you like him. I found him boring." "You got Dr. Bonedry for Biology. I pity you!" "She's a neat person. You'll like her as a counselor. She helped me a lot."

I recall a college friend of mine who once signed up for a class taught by a professor who had a poor reputation as a teacher. My friend told me, "Norm, I'm determined to go into the class believing that this man has much to teach me. I refuse to be conditioned against him by others." Toward the end of the semester he affirmed that he found many helpful insights from the "poor" teacher. Perhaps his refusal to be prejudiced by fellow students was the deciding factor.

A counselor friend once told me of a lady who came to

him describing her husband as a barbarous brute—unreasonable, disgusting, and uncooperative. When the husband came for counseling, my friend was amazed to find that the man was a cooperative, "civilized" person. My friend had been led to believe something inconsistent with later facts.

Question 3: What are my expectations? What information do I expect to receive from this person? My friend Meri MacLeod recently attended a conference for her personal enrichment. The literature she received and the comments of friends who were familiar with the speakers had led her to expect a stimulating and helpful experience. After the conference she said, "Because my expectations were not met in some seminars, I found it difficult to pay attention to certain of the speakers. I expected them to be stimulating and creative in their presentations, but I discovered they were repeating what they had written in their books. It turned me off."

Being aware of our expectations can help us realize when they influence our listening. If expectations are not being met, perhaps they can be adjusted to achieve realistic benefits and make the best of the situation for all involved.

Make It Pleasurable to Share Ideas

I distinctly remember one of my early preaching experiences. I was a young man struggling to learn to preach effectively. I had prayed and prepared diligently for this particular sermon, and I stood before my audience with fear and trembling, desperately desiring their encouragement and acceptance. As I gazed at my audience I was struck by the lack of response. The "stone faces" I encountered only heightened my uneasiness as I preached before them.

A few days later the Lord encouraged my heart as I read of the young man Jeremiah's encouragement from the Lord.

Jeremiah appeared to have experienced what I had encountered:

> Then said I, Ah, Lord God! behold, I cannot speak; for I am a child. But the Lord said unto me, Say not, I am a child; for thou shalt go to all that I shall send thee, and whatsoever I command thee thou shalt speak. *Be not afraid of their faces; for I am with thee to deliver thee,* saith the Lord (Jer. 1:6–8, KJV, italics mine).

In the years that have passed since that experience, I have come to see that listeners can do a number of things to encourage speakers. In the process, they may make the act of listening more pleasurable, since an encouraged speaker is a more relaxed, personable, and interesting speaker.

Here are some ways a listener can facilitate the process of sharing ideas:

1) *Determine to look attentive and eager.* A pleasant look encourages a speaker. The powerful preacher, Charles H. Spurgeon, once said, "To me it is an annoyance if even a blind man does not look me in the face." [1] Whether we are sitting across the table while a friend tells of an irritating problem he is trying to resolve, or listening while the manager shares company goals, our attentiveness will enhance the communication process.

2) *Express appreciation verbally.* Affirmative responses like "What you said was helpful. Thanks for sharing it," or "I'd never heard that concept before. It is what I've needed to resolve my problem," encourage individuals to continue speaking. A person who sees his ideas as worthwhile and appreciated will be motivated to share more. If you appreciate what a speaker says, say so!

3) *Participate with the speaker.* Participation may be either verbal or nonverbal. Verbal participation includes raising questions or making comments: it may be a simple statement

such as "I agree," "Yes," and "That's helpful." Nonverbal participation may include a smile, a nod of approval, an attentive look. All of these express interest in what the speaker is communicating.

4) *Don't interrupt.* Interrupting cuts off the flow of information. It inhibits the flow of the speaker's thoughts and communicates, "I don't want to listen to you." For some listeners, not interrupting may require the self-discipline of waiting to speak and the self-examination of determining whether they are planning a response rather than attending to the speaker.

How to Listen for Information

Stan and Frieda have a problem which has persisted for the five years of their marriage: Frieda's habit of leaving things around the house continually bothers Stan, who likes things neat. It's not a difficult problem to resolve, yet it hangs on, irritating them, sapping the vitality of their relationship. Somehow they can't use their resources to find a solution.

What counsel can we give our two friends? What practical actions can help them listen to each other for ideas and information and then work together to reach a solution to their difficulty? Here are several guidelines for solving problems by listening for ideas:

1) *Spiritual, physical, mental, and environmental preparation.* The first step Stan and Frieda need to take is to prepare themselves to listen to each other. Spiritual preparation is foundational for good listening; heart preparation through prayer opens us up to the resources of the Holy Spirit. Setting aside time to listen to God is helpful in preparing for listening to one another.

Physical preparation is another essential for listening. Physical weariness—or hunger or thirst—can decrease mental alertness and hamper listening. Sometimes we need rest or food before we're prepared to listen.

Mental preparation is necessary, too. Other thoughts, concerns, and emotions may be vying for attention and need to be put aside. We need to know ahead of time what information we will need and what we should listen for.

Finally, environmental preparation is profitable. What location would be best for the discussion? Where could we listen with the least distraction? Do we habitually sit in the back of the auditorium where all those in front of us can distract us? When we listen in a one-to-one relationship, do we find a location which is private and comfortable, and which allows us to have eye contact with the person speaking?

2) *Concentrate on the other as communicator.* Our friends Stan and Frieda will hear each other's ideas better if they view each other in a nontypical way—"View the others in a discussion as sources of ideas and information, not as personalities." [2] If we are concentrating on a speaker in a wrong way, our receptivity to his or her insights and ideas will be reduced; rather than viewing the other person as communicator, we may see him or her socially ("He's beneath me"), educationally ("She doesn't know as much as I do because she never attended college"), sexually ("She's not bright; she's a woman"), or physically ("I'm bigger than he is").

3) *Learn to give feedback effectively.* This is something Stan and Frieda may need to learn. The word, *feedback,* refers to the listener's practice of repeating to the speaker what he has heard the speaker say. Feedback may also include nonverbal information of which the speaker is not aware ("When you point your finger at me I feel accused"). Giving

and receiving feedback allows the speaker and listener to compare their understandings, clarify misunderstandings, and monitor progress. It is an essential feature of listening for information.

4) *Use analytical skills to supplement listening.* Our friends may need to learn how to think actively along with the speaker and to analyze the data the speaker is providing. But a word of caution is needed at this point. Becoming too analytical can keep a listener from hearing what is being said. He may become so involved in his own thought processes that he misses important information being given.

5) *Take notes on key points.* It might help Stan and Frieda to jot down key information that comes out in their discussions. It helps to make brief notes of essential ideas we don't want to forget; doing this aids in keeping information before us. But I emphasize *key* information. Taking too elaborate notes can also distract a listener from what the speaker is saying.

In many of our relationships we are continually giving and receiving information. It is to our advantage to develop our listenability so that we profit from the information available to us. By practicing the concepts outlined in this chapter we can listen more effectively for ideas. In the process, we will help not only those to whom we listen, but ourselves as well.

It's Your Turn

To gain practical benefits from this chapter, it is important to apply the concepts to your listening relationships. The activities on the following page are designed to help you in this process.

1. Review question #1 on p. 33. Beside each factor on the list, jot down the name of someone to whom you would have difficulty in listening objectively because of that factor. For example, if you were fifty years old, to what young adult (aged eighteen to twenty-five) would you have difficulty listening? If possible put down names of people you would really encounter (rather than national personalities). It is important for this exercise to identify people we typically "turn off."

2. Place a check in the appropriate box if you practice the skill described in the situation listed:

I consciously *prepare* myself to listen.	□ *study groups* □ *S.s. class* □ *sermon* □ *news report* □ *other*
I concentrate on the speaker as a *communicator*.	□ *study groups* □ *S.s. class* □ *sermon* □ *news report* □ *other*
I give feedback effectively when possible	□ *study groups* □ *S.s. class* □ *sermon* □ *news report* □ *other*

I *actively* think along with the speaker, using *analytical skills*.	☐ *study groups* ☐ *S.s. class* ☐ *sermon* ☐ *news report* ☐ *other*
I jot down *notes* of key ideas I want to remember.	☐ *study groups* ☐ *S.s. class* ☐ *sermon* ☐ *news report* ☐ *other*

five

REACHING A
SHARED MEANING

MOST OF US HAVE SEEN the little motto that frequently appears on cards and posters: "I know you believe you understand what you think I said, but I am not sure you realize that what you heard is not what I meant." While we chuckle at the statement, it makes a point: communication between the sender and receiver is frequently distorted—without one or both persons knowing it.

The risk of misunderstanding or being misunderstood increases when little or no opportunity is given for dialogue, feedback, and clarification. When there *is* the chance to clarify the speaker's ideas and check the accuracy of what has been heard, certain specific listening skills can help the communication process.

Some time ago, Winnie and I were invited to attend a series of workshops led by Dallas and Nancy Demmitt. These two delightful people possess remarkable insight into communication skills. Working as a husband-wife team, they invest their teaching-counseling abilities in helping other couples communicate effectively. My wife and I were impressed with the potential of this ministry to transform struggling relationships.

One concept they shared that we found especially valuable is that of "shared meaning." As we worked through the process of "reaching a shared meaning," we could see that it is a valuable tool for increasing accuracy of communication and deepening any close relationship. The Demmitts introduced us to the book *Alive and Aware*,[1] which enriched our understanding of the concept even more. In this chapter I would like to use the idea of shared meaning to help you gain insight for your listening growth.

Checking Out

The entire shared-meaning process is built on a basic listening skill—that of "checking out" what a speaker is saying. When we check out a message, we share our perception of what we have heard with the speaker, and give him or her the chance to confirm the accuracy of what we have understood or correct any distortions in the message. Here's an example of checking out a statement:

> MARK: "I feel frustrated when you leave the newspapers in different rooms of the house and I have to search all over to find them. I'd like you to be considerate of my needs."
> BETTY: "I need to check out what I am hearing you say. I hear you say that you're upset because I don't put the newspapers in one place. You want me to be considerate of your needs. Is that what you said?"
> MARK: "That's right."

There are many reasons why checking out communication is an important listening skill. In the first place, it is easy for listeners to misinterpret what a speaker says. In communication seminars I frequently project this statement on an overhead screen: "I didn't say you were stupid." I then ask the participants what the statement is intended to mean.

the kitchen and said, 'Winnie, is something wrong?' You heard my nonverbal message!"

We laughed together and I thanked her for such a relevant illustration with which to end this chapter!

Enriching Your Understanding

To help you apply the concepts described in this chapter, I suggest that you work through the following exercises. They will increase your sensitivity to nonverbal behavior.

---

1. Turn on your television set, but leave the volume off. Choose a program which portrays people communicating in life situations. In a notebook, jot down nonverbal behaviors you observe and what messages they might be communicating. If possible, do this viewing with another person; then compare your perceptions.

2. Discuss what nonverbal behaviors a person might display if he or she is feeling:

   a. nervous   g. rejected
   b. happy   h. loved
   c. fearful   i. insecure
   d. angry   j. inferior
   e. lonely   k. bored
   f. shy   l. secure

eight

QUESTIONS: THE LISTENER'S FRIEND

"The question is a remarkable conversation instrument."[1] This deceptively simple device has the power to control another's thought processes—pointing out deficiencies, leading into new pathways of thought, probing motives, attitudes, prejudices.

Let me demonstrate the power of a question to control the mind. Consider this question: What is the sixth book of the Old Testament? Now dismiss the question from your mind. Chances are, you won't be able to do it. Something in your thought process pushes you to respond. You cannot leave it unanswered, even though you know the question is unimportant. The brain demands that you complete the process.

Are you committed to being a more effective listener? Do you want to discover the ministry of listening? Then you'll want to learn to use questions skillfully. Questions are powerful tools in the hands of a skillful listener. They equip him with power to probe the speaker's thoughts, keep him involved in a dialogue, and guide the thought process in a profitable direction.

When Questions Fail

I have exalted the question to a place of dignity and respect. Yet, it often falls into disgrace and disuse. When used unwisely or carelessly, the question is disarmed—robbed of power. Let's consider the *ineffective* use of the question.

Questions lose their power when they are *poorly worded.* Poorly worded questions create confusion. I recall a fellow graduate student who struggled with the use of questions. He would state his question. Then he would explain and embellish the question until we were sufficiently confused and unable to answer it. I soon learned that answering my friend's questions was too much trouble, because it was so difficult to find out what he wanted to know!

Questions lose their power when they are *the wrong kind.* The most powerful questions are those that affect our lives. Wrong questions are those which pursue irrelevant material and lead others down dead-end streets. Effective listeners ask questions that are designed to aid the speaker—not satisfy the listener's curiosity.

When the *speaker answers his own questions,* those questions lose their potential to initiate thought. I once had a Sunday school teacher who adopted this practice. He would ask questions, but never gave us time to respond. This practice frustrated me; it also caused me to lose interest in his questions, because I knew he wouldn't let me get actively involved.

Some questions are weak and anemic because they are *thoughtless*—they are asked too casually and without careful thought. Powerful questions are carefully chosen. Through practice, skillful listeners can learn to form questions quickly, but they also learn how to do this wisely. An inexperienced listener will probably have to take more time to plan the choice of questions more carefully.

If *too many* questions are used, they lose their impact. Too many questions can make others feel uncomfortable and defensive, as though they were being grilled. In general conversation, people want to enter into dialogue with each other. Questions should be interspersed with personal sharing, so that each conversational partner feels that he is sharing of himself.

Six Ways Questions Can Serve Us

When skillfully used, the question is a very versatile device, able to serve many functions. It is very useful for getting clarification from a speaker: "I'm uncertain about what you meant when you said 'I'm ambivalent.' Could you clarify that for me?" Questions such as these cue the speaker to any confusion and let him know when to pause and explain more carefully.

Questions also enable listeners to reflect back what they have heard a speaker say. This helps both speaker and listener match their perceptions to see if they are on the same track. The key to using reflective questions is to feed back the essential words of the message: "I'm hearing you say that you are discouraged with your poor sales record. Is that correct?" When we give feedback as to what we're hearing, the other person can affirm or correct what we've reflected in our question.

Questions are an invaluable help in collecting vital information. They help us find out facts we need to discover about the other person or the problem before us. Questions like these can build relationships by helping us gather essential information for mutual problem solving.

In our church family gatherings, we frequently use questions as a means to help Christians learn about each other. Questions initiate conversations that lead to personal sharing. In this way we have continued to grow in our knowledge of one another. This practice has helped break down barriers of alienation and enabled fellow Christians to discover common interests that enrich their relationships.

Jesse Nirenberg offers us valuable insight in the use of questions to gain information. He notes that questions range from high-structured to low-structured. A highly structured question is used to gain specific information: "What is your favorite food?" Low-structured questions seek more general information and invite the speaker to share more freely: "How have your parents' attitudes toward food influenced you?" Notice that the low-structured questions gives the responder much more freedom to reply in a variety of ways. Nirenberg stresses that low-structured questions are likely to produce more information from the speaker. Thus, if our goal is to encourage the speaker or to get more information, we would use the low-structured question.[2] Often, it is wise to plan in advance the question we want to ask.

Questions can serve us in another way—by helping us confront another person. Jesus used a confronting question when he asked Nicodemus, "Are you the teacher of Israel, and do not understand these things?" (John 3:10, NASB). We may phrase questions to confront an individual either directly or indirectly. A direct question might be, "Why did you lie to me about where you were?" A more indirect question might be, "I felt upset when I found you'd lied to me. Can we talk about it?" Indirect questions will probably get at the same issue, but may be less threatening to the other person.

Questions are invaluable for still another reason. They serve well in stimulating the spirit of inquiry. Provocative questions motivate others to more serious thought. When we use questions wisely, we are able to guide the thinking processes of an individual or group; we hold the initiative.

As a matter of fact, we can *control* the group process by the skillful use of questions.

Used in a negative way, questions can put another on the defensive—have you ever felt "backed into a corner" by someone's persistent questions? But my emphasis here is intended to be positive. The wise question is like a rudder on a ship; it determines the direction of thought and conversation.

Here's one final reason I encourage the skillful use of questions: they are great ways to lead people to apply truth and clarify values. Effective questions can stimulate growth. A powerful illustration is found in the life of Jesus Christ. In Matthew 16:13–16, Jesus raises two questions to his disciples:

> When Jesus came to the region of Caesarea Philippi, he asked his disciples, "Who do people say the Son of Man is?"
> They replied, "Some say John the Baptist; others say Elijah; and still others, Jeremiah or one of the prophets."
> "But what about you?" he asked. "Who do you say I am?"
> Simon Peter answered, "You are the Christ, the Son of the living God."

In raising these two simple but powerful questions, Jesus led Peter to express his faith that Jesus was the Messiah. No doubt this was the first time Peter had verbalized his growing conviction.

When we use questions for the purpose of values-clarification, we attempt to raise value-laden questions that aid an individual in examining or articulating his or her values. Value-oriented questions are especially powerful in provoking thought about personal values.

Questions are also a fundamental tool in helping individuals apply new concepts to their lives. "What would be the first step in applying this principle to your life?" "If you were to practice this teaching, what changes would you make?"—questions like these have the potential to initiate change in the individual.

Can you see why I count the question as one of my close friends in listening? Perhaps you see why Nirenberg said, "The question is a remarkable conversation instrument." Why not consider anew how this provocative tool can help you as a communicator? What new strength could it contribute to your interpersonal skills?

Ways to Honor the Question

I have said that questions are ineffective when used carelessly, but invaluable when used carefully, wisely, and skillfully. If we want questions to serve us, we must treat them with the dignity that gives them power. To do so, it will be helpful to investigate several guidelines for the effective use of questions:

1) *Phrase questions simply, directly, and clearly.* Observe Christ's use of questions. They are remarkably simple, pointedly direct, and very clear:

"How can Satan drive out Satan?" (Mark 3:23).
"Who are my mother and my brothers?" (Mark 3:33).
"Why are you so afraid? Do you still have no faith?" (Mark 4:40).
"Are your hearts hardened?" (Mark 8:17).
"What did Moses command you?" (Mark 10:3).
"What do you want me to do for you?" (Mark 10:36).

Notice how concise these questions are. Long, involved, wordy questions confuse people. By the time they have unraveled the question to find what we're asking, their motivation to reply has diminished. And the sluggish listener will not bother to seek a clarification; he'll go to sleep!

Many people assume that anyone can ask an effective question without practice. Not true! For several years I instructed seminary students in teaching methods. I found the students consistently weak in phrasing good questions until they practiced applying the principles of simplicity, directness, and clarity.

A good exercise for increasing effectiveness in asking questions is to write out the questions before asking them. Chop out needless phrases. Simplify them. Make them easy to grasp the first time they are heard.

When you are involved as a listener, *think carefully* about the question you want to ask. Some people find it helpful to keep a notepad or three-by-five cards to jot down questions they plan to use. Give yourself ample time to think through the question you want to ask. Will it get the information you want? Will it entice the other person to think more deeply?

2) *Start conversations with easy questions.* Use questions that the other person does not have to think deeply about. The first couple of minutes of a relationship are the most awkward; using questions that invite a ready response gives the other person confidence, and helps him relax.

A good principle is to begin conversations with low-structured questions and move to high-structured (if you need specific data) as the relationship becomes established. Since the low-structured question gives the speaker more freedom of response, he is more likely to relax and feel comfortable. This is true whether we are meeting new friends, interviewing someone for a job, or establishing initial rapport with a counselee.

3) *Use "yes" and "no" questions sparingly.* Such questions do not tend to involve the person significantly or to stimulate creative inquiry. Neither do they usually provide us with any significant insight. If we are trying to gain information about the individual with whom we are speaking, we will

use questions which encourage him or her to share more fully.

Also be cautious about using "why" questions. When focusing on interpersonal problems, "why" questions often give little or no help in resolving the problem. Asking "Why did you do it?" may not be as helpful as asking, "What could we do to resolve the problem?" or "What are you willing to do to establish a healthier relationship with your sister?" The "why" questions often are less solution-oriented than "what" or "how" questions.

4) *Practice answering a question with a question.* It may be flattering to hear another say, "Will you do this for me?", but it may be more helpful to respond, "What do you see as the first step?" and then to guide the individual in working through the solution himself. A principle I have tried to apply is to never do for the other person what he can *more profitably* do for himself. This applies to answering questions. If it is more profitable for the other person to think, analyze, and inquire, then we should consider the profit of answering his questions with a question:

"Before I answer I'd like to know what you think."
"How would you answer the question?"
"I wonder how the rest of you would respond to Jo's question."

An underlying conviction of the book is that listening can be a ministry for the Christian. The wise listener wants to respond to the speaker in a way that will promote that person's growth and insight. In some cases, answering a question with a question may be the most appropriate means of reaching this goal. This is especially true when the person we are relating to has the habit of allowing others to do his thinking for him. Our goal can be to excite him about the challenge of personal discovery.

Once we have asked the question, it is important to allow ample time for the individual—or group—to respond. Many people become nervous or impatient if their questions are not answered immediately. But silence is an indication that someone is thinking! If the question is worth asking, it is worth allowing the person of whom it is asked ample opportunity to ponder his or her response.

5) *In a group situation, ask the question first; then direct it to an individual* if you want an individual response. This tactic is more educationally sound than directing the question to the individual first, because it keeps the entire group involved. When only one individual is questioned, others may turn off their thought processes: "He's asking Jeff. I can relax and not think about it."

6) *Avoid questions that attack.* Questions can be used to ridicule, attack, embarrass, or belittle an individual:

"Don't you know any better than to do that?"
"Why did you do such a foolish thing?"
"Don't you realize a Christian shouldn't think such thoughts?"

Such questions do damage to the person and cause him to withdraw from interaction. But our purpose in questioning should always be to build up, to edify the other person—not tear him down.

An excellent biblical principle is contained in Ephesians 4:29: "Do not let any unwholesome talk come out of your mouths, but only what is helpful for building others up according to their needs, that it may benefit those who listen." We are challenged to make all of our speech positive, constructive, and wholesome. Every expression from our lips can be a ministry of the indwelling Spirit. The questions we ask others are a valuable means of applying the principle contained in this verse.

Developing Questioning Skills

I have stressed the need for using questions effectively. This requires skill. For practice, analyze the questions that follow.

Read each question carefully. Decide whether it is effective or ineffective. Circle the ineffective questions. Beside them, jot down *why* they are ineffective (too long, too complex, attack the speaker, poorly worded, nonstimulating, etc.). Try to rewrite them to make them more effective.

1. "Al, if this questioning business is important, and I'm sure it is, should we elaborate on those factors which facilitate direct bridges to more skillful wording or just better sentences?"
2. "You're not feeling well?"
3. "Why should John stay home and you get to go? Is that fair?"
4. "What in this chapter could be misconstrued as being an apparent attack upon the reliability of the reader to assimilate verbal content?"
5. "Apparently you've made up your mind to have your own way—right?"
6. "Should every Christian pray?"
7. "Does John 17 indicate that it is more important to stand or kneel when praying?"
8. "What have I been doing that's aggravated your anger toward me?"
9. "Would you expand on point three? It's still unclear."
10. "Why don't you sell your car to pay the debt?"
11. "You think you're better than I, don't you?"
12. "I'm upset. Could we talk about this later?"

nine

LISTENING FOR PERSONAL GROWTH

Perceptive listening is a ministry to others, but it can also be a way to minister to ourselves. Sensitive, careful listening helps us gain fuller insight into ourselves and into our relationships with others.

After all, listening is one of the primary means we have for learning about ourselves. As children, we develop our perceptions of who we are and what we are destined to become largely according to what our parents say about us: "I like you"; "You're a helpful child"; "You're such a crybaby." As we grow older, other voices add to those perceptions, complementing or challenging what our parents have said.

Gradually, we learn to filter out what we do not want to hear, to modify what is incongruent with our self-perception, to absorb data which seems useful. But all through life we remain dependent on outside input to help us see and understand who we are and where we are going. When we listen with discernment—to God, to other people, even to our inner selves—we grow. We discover valuable truths that help us move toward wholeness. We come to see our strengths and the areas in which we need to change. Listening can move us toward the fullness of what God intended for our lives.

Listening to God

Our God is not silent. He speaks. Nowhere is this more powerfully stated than in the words of John 1:1: "In the beginning was the Word, and the Word was with God, and the Word was God." The Father spoke clearly, powerfully, and intimately through Jesus Christ. Even now, he voices his personal testimony of his nature. He expresses his profound concern for each of us. He says, "I love you."

A. W. Tozer underscores this truth when he writes, "The facts are that God is not silent, has never been silent. It is the nature of God to speak."[1] He speaks, not only that we might know him, but that we might clearly understand ourselves and our relationship to him. He addresses us so that our lives may come into intimate relationship with him. In this growing intimacy we are drawn to maturity.

God wants us to listen to him. He gains no satisfaction from uninformed children. Jesus said, "He who has ears, let him hear" (Matt. 11:15). Unfortunately, we do not always heed his invitation. Isaiah lamented the refusal of Israel to hear God's voice urging them to repentance and personal growth. Jeremiah and Ezekiel joined him in expressing God's concern that his people would not listen (Isa. 6:9; Jer. 5:21; Ezek. 12:2). Jesus applied the same truth to the Jews of his day. Their ears were deaf to those life-changing truths he longed to impart to them. They could not hear God's voice (Mark 8:18).

We can profit from the counsel of Scripture by recognizing the danger of not hearing God's voice. We can be alert to the fact that the noise of self-interest, distractions, and daily activities can muffle the Father's counsel and instruction.

This brings us to several important questions: How do we listen to God? Can we learn to know he is speaking? How does he express himself?

We know that our Father has spoken and continues to speak through the Scriptures. They are the fundamental means he has chosen to communicate his life principles to his children. The Scriptures contain the words of life. Jesus said, "The words I have spoken to you are spirit and they are life" (John 6:63). Christ's words have life-changing potential. As we listen perceptively and apply what he says to our lives, our speaking God transforms us through his wisdom and power. Thus, alertness to hear and to act upon what he voices is of critical importance.

God has designed a process for our growth that involves listening. The sequence of the process is: (1) He speaks, (2) I listen, (3) I believe, (4) I apply, (5) I am changed (see John 5:24; 15:3). The essential dynamics of transformation are embodied in this process, which brings a cleansing from defeat patterns, and growth in intimate relationship to our heavenly Father (John 15:3; 17:17).

A practical implication of God speaking through the Scriptures is that we need to listen to him there. If we are convinced that he seeks relationship, we will set aside time to meet him in a listening, meditative spirit. Many

Christians are defeated at this point because they view Bible reading as a duty rather than an opportunity; it becomes a chore rather than a joy, a burden rather than a delight. The correct mental attitude is crucial to listening to Scripture in a life-changing manner.

One day while I was teaching in seminary, a student came to my office. This man, who served on the pastoral staff of a local church, had already received an M.Div. degree from the seminary, but had returned to take courses in Christian education to enrich his ministry. Here is what he said:

"Norm, personal Bible study is a constant frustration to me. When I try to do it I get turned off. I can prepare sermons and teach Bible classes, but when it comes to studying the Bible for personal growth, I am defeated."

During the conversation that followed, I discovered that my friend had come to see the Bible as a college and seminary textbook to master. The personal message from a compassionate God was clouded by term papers and exams analyzing context, translations, and so on. Bit by bit, this love letter from God had become a manual to be mastered; it had lost its delight.

Together, we mapped out a strategy for Bible study, in which he was to spend time with a modern translation away from his office, rediscovering a personal, relational approach to the Scripture. In the weeks that followed, he learned again how to sit in God's presence and enter into an intimate dialogue with his Father, and he began once again to relish those precious encounters with God.

Though the Bible is a primary means by which God speaks to us, it is not the only source. Tozer notes,

> The Bible is the written word of God, and because it is written it is confined and limited by the necessities of ink and paper and leather. The Voice of God, however, is alive and free as the sovereign God is free.[2]

This brings us to a second way that we can listen to God. He speaks to us through the indwelling Spirit. The very presence of the Holy Spirit is evidence that God is relating to us. This fact is clearly conveyed by Jesus' words in John 14:26: "But the Counselor, the Holy Spirit, whom the Father will send in my name, will teach you all things and will remind you of everything I have said to you." Our Father nurtures us through the counsel of the indwelling One if we listen to him. How essential it is that we know how to hear the voice of God; how vital it is to our growth.

Several years ago our family moved from Portsmouth, Virginia, to Wheaton, Illinois, where I was to pursue graduate studies. We loaded our belongings into a Falcon station wagon and large U-Haul trailer. By the time we had traveled fifty miles of our eight-hundred-mile trip, I knew the automobile would not be able to pull the trailer that distance. I felt a deep sense of inadequacy and helplessness. What was I to do? I could not turn back, yet the journey ahead was in jeopardy. All that night and the following day I felt emotionally drained. Finally, with the support and counsel of my father-in-law, Wilfred Townsend, we decided to rent a U-Haul truck instead of a trailer and made the move in two vehicles.

The next day, Sunday, I attended the services of Immanuel Baptist Church in Richmond, Virginia. The Spirit of God ministered to me in a significant way. I sensed his presence and support through each hymn we sang. As I heard him speak, I was overwhelmed and wept with gratitude.

Many times and in many circumstances we hear God's quiet, compassionate voice. So frequently he counsels us in his own unique way. Often he encourages us to take the next step that leads to new dimensions of growth. Learning to sense his presence and know his voice is critical. Developing our own ability to hear him is vital to the enrichment of our lives.

Thus, we grow by listening to God. As we listen and respond positively, we are changed—changed into his likeness.

We return to our friend Tozer and affirm his prayer as that of our own:

> Lord, teach me to listen. The times are noisy and my ears are weary with the thousand raucous sounds which continuously assault them. Give me the spirit of the boy Samuel when he said to Thee, "Speak, for thy servant heareth." Let me hear Thee speaking in my heart. Let me get used to the sound of Thy Voice, that its tones may be familiar when the sounds of earth die away and the only sound will be the music of Thy speaking Voice. Amen.[3]

Listening to Others

Are you aware of the hidden you—those habits, mannerisms, idiosyncrasies which others see, though you do not? We all have a part of us that's known to others but hidden from ourselves. There's nothing wrong with that; the trouble comes when we need to see ourselves as others see us, but are unable to do so. Sometimes it's because others are afraid to tell us; they think we would get angry, tell them to mind their own business, break off our friendship. Thus, we never get valuable information which could enrich us.

We all need feedback—essential information about ourselves given us by others. Feedback enables us to monitor who we are and what we are doing.

Feedback is necessary because it complements the subjective view we have of ourselves. It supplements information we presently have. Sometimes feedback comes in the form of a performance evaluation, test results, job evaluation. At other times, feedback comes when friends or family members share their perspective on a problem we are coping with, telling us how they see us handling it, obstacles we have overlooked, or progress they feel is occurring.

Feedback that facilitates personal growth is usually most effective when the interpersonal relationship is strong. Warm, caring relationships foster an environment that is conducive to open, honest feedback. As we grow in loving concern for one another, we want to share insights which will enrich each other's life. One reason many people never see the hidden part of their lives is that they avoid the kind of relationships that would reveal this to them.

What can others reveal to us about our hidden selves? What information can be given to us for our profit? Let me suggest three possibilities. First, others can give us *details* about ourselves. The facts may be neither good nor bad, but they are invaluable to us in gaining a fuller self-portrait. For instance, I have observed that my son, Joel, is action-oriented; he does not sit still long, and he becomes bored easily. I know that my daughter, Jill, is warm and affectionate; she is also more hesitant to act, waiting for others to begin. These basic bits of information about two of my children may shed light on how they cope with life situations. Sharing this information with them can be valuable for their self-growth.

Second, others can show us our *strengths*. I observe that many of us hesitate to trust our own subjective evaluations of ourselves; for example, we hesitate to declare enthusiastically, "I am a gifted teacher. I feel very happy about it." But others can point out factual data which affirms our own perception of the skills, talents, or gifts we possess. Such feedback reinforces our growing awareness of our inner potential.

This point must be underscored for both speaker and listener. Most people will be helped significantly in their personal growth when we affirm the valid strengths we see in them. Ephesians 4:29 states, "Do not let unwholesome talk come out of your mouths, but only what is helpful for building others up . . . that it may benefit those who listen." Wise feedback is a powerful means of building others up by validating their strengths. One of the immense benefits of small sharing groups is the potential of encouraging and affirming positive growth in the members' lives.

Some time ago my friend, Ted Sellers, shared an observation with me. He said, "Norm, I believe you have the gift of faith. You are visionary. You see possibilities and opportunities others don't." Ted's thoughtful remarks were very provocative to me. I came away from our conversation pondering what he had said. Ted's words helped me grow.

Feedback from others can reveal to us a third dimension of our lives. Others can point out *areas of need* and weakness in our lives—areas we have not faced. I recall hearing a denominational leader describe his encounter with a pastor who had developed a consistently negative attitude. Church members complained of his refusal to listen to new ideas, and of his tendency to criticize and judge other people. Through the leader's wise and gentle feedback, this pastor came to grips with his area of need. The apostle Paul describes a similar situation in which he challenged Peter about an inconsistency in his life. He says, "When Peter came to Antioch, I opposed him to his face, because he was in the wrong" (Gal. 2:11). In other words, Paul gave Peter feedback.

Consider what has been said. We listen to others to receive their perspective on our life, to see what they see. This is essential for healthy self-growth. We should carefully consider what our husband or wife says about us. We should listen thoughtfully when our children say, "Dad (or Mom), did you realize that you . . ." We should pause and reflect when a work associate points out a strength or weakness he sees. These people are helping us to see ourselves more fully.

Unfortunately, some people never profit from feedback. Some are defensive. They argue rather than listen; they defend themselves rather than hear. Such people go through life sweeping valuable information under a mental carpet, pushing it from view. They would rather keep their hidden-self out of their sight than face it as a growing challenge. Some secretly know that what is being reported to them is true but outwardly deny it. Others may honestly not see the problem or opportunity before them and consistently reject sound counsel.

Defensiveness can be a barrier to self-growth. Another barrier is low self-esteem. Low self-esteem is a deadly enemy to many Christians' growth. Because they continue to believe the lie that "I am stupid," "I am incompetent," "I am ugly," and so on, they cannot believe the truth about themselves that others point out. They continue living defeated lives, believing that they are rejects, incompetent, deficient. The positive qualities others see in them are cast aside because those qualities do not fit the image these individuals have of themselves. They do not listen to learn.

I have not meant to imply that we should unquestioningly accept everything others say about us. If what another person says is true, he or she should be able to document it with clear facts. Then we should look at those facts honestly. In addition, we can seek the perspective of still another person who may be able to add insight or correct the first person's observations.

Look at it this way. Imagine yourself going to a physician for an examination. After the check-up he reports, "You have leukemia." Your mind reels; it seems impossible. You ask for facts—"How do you know I have this hateful disease?" He gives the results of two highly accurate tests he has administered.

You face a choice—accept the facts and begin the necessary treatment, or deny the facts and continue to die. You may seek another medical opinion, but if the second doctor agrees with the first you will again be called to face the situation and to change your life accordingly.

Throughout life we have the opportunity to listen and learn about ourselves. Feedback from others is vital for personal growth. What we do with that information may be even more strategic.

Listening to Self

hidden from me
known to God

hidden
from
conscious
me

LISTENING

hidden
from me

known to
others

known to my
inner self

Some of the most creative moments of my life have been those times when I have sat in solitude on a hillside, or ambled through a grove of towering pines listening to nothing but my innermost thoughts.[4]

This statement by Robert A. Williams underscores the value of quiet, reflective times when we can get in touch with the movements of our lives. These are the times when we listen to ourselves—to the inner voice that is often drowned out in the bustle of everyday life. These occasions may lead to a reappraisal of our lifestyle, an inventory of our activities, or a commitment to face a challenge.

As we take private time to think, pray, or plan we may discover many things. Often, when we take time to listen to our inner voice, we find an internal process that has been underway for some time. We may get in touch with *visions* we have carried for years—unfulfilled dreams that could enrich, even revolutionize, our lives. These challenges might be as incredible as sailing across the Atlantic in a ten-foot sailboat or as life-changing as returning to college to study a new field that intrigues us.

Sometimes as we listen to our inner voice, we come in touch with a *complaint* we have not faced. We may realize that our marriage relationship is deteriorating through neglect, that an intense work schedule has choked off meaningful time spent with our partner. We may hear a voice calling us to reevaluate our priorities and to take action.

The inner voice may tell us of a *pattern of life* which needs to be altered through God's power. Perhaps we've developed the habit of shutting other people out of our lives because we fear involvement. We may ponder, "Is it too late for me to change? Or could I begin to grow in facing the fear, in discovering the joy of relationships?"

Listening to ourselves—to the inner voice—involves making two decisions. The first decision is to seek out moments of silence for personal reflection, meditation, and growth.

This practice is not common to our culture. Most of us have no plan for quiet spaces in our lives. The typical American's life is surrounded by noise and confusion. *We must deliberately choose to seek out silence and plan it into our daily activity.*

I believe that it is healthy for each Christian to budget time daily for a minimum of fifteen minutes of personal reflection and meditation. During that time, we should try to sense the issues and concerns that we are grappling with internally. We should try to focus on them as clearly as possible and sense what we are being called to do.

I must stress the importance of silence. This may appear obvious, but it is crucial; to listen to our inner selves, we must find a place as quiet as possible. These moments of meditation are to be a time of personal reflection, appraisal, and growth. It may be helpful to keep a diary or journal of insights and thoughts which come to mind.

The second decision necessary for listening to our inner selves is the decision to act. Personal growth is typically an act of faith. It requires a step in a new direction, opening a new chapter in our lives, attempting something we have never tried before, conquering a hurdle that seems impossibly high. As we interact with God about these inner concerns, we will inevitably be led to a faith decision: "Through God's indwelling power, I will accept the challenge before me to step out in a new venture of growth." [4]

I was discussing this chapter with my friend Meri Mac-Leod, and she pointed out the cyclic nature of this process. The diagram below illustrates the cycle:

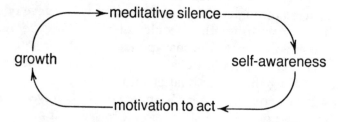

Through times of meditative silence, we become self-aware. As we become self-aware and interact with the Spirit of God, we are inevitably brought to a decision point. Will we act? Will we draw upon God's resources and our own resources to act upon this new challenge before us? Dialogue with the indwelling Spirit will engender motivation. As we act in faith, pursuing the challenge, we grow. However, the process does not end here. The new-found growth leads to new insight, which is fed into new times of meditative silence, which leads to greater self-awareness, and so on. The cycle continues to *expand,* because each new growth experience provides us with new creative resources, as well as new awareness.

Thus, we can see the potential for three dynamic processes operating in our lives as we become skilled listeners. We hear the voice of God—guiding, teaching, enriching, and affirming us. We hear the voices of other people providing invaluable input for our growth processes. Finally, we recognize an internal voice of the self making us aware of important life issues we can tackle. These three processes, when functioning healthily, provide incredible potential to stretch, nurture, enrich—yes, even revolutionize our lives.

Responding for Personal Growth

Personal growth—that's what this chapter is all about. Personal growth comes through the application of truths we are discovering. Thus, it is important for us to respond to what we are learning. The following exercises will guide you in that process.

---

1. Earlier I asked, "How do we listen to God?" I'd like you to respond to that personally. Jot down several ways

that you typically listen to God. Then reflect on what you have read in this chapter. Have other ways been suggested? If so, add them to your list and consider how to put them into practice.

2. Helping others grow is as important as our own growth. The chart below will help you think through strengths you see in your family members and friends. Plan specific ways to affirm their strengths (note in mail, phone call, personal visit, etc.).

Person   *Strength*

_____   _____

_____   _____

_____   _____

_____   _____

3. Complete the following statement: The time and place I will reserve for personal meditation are _____
_____

4. Jot down facts related to personal growth that you already know about yourself. About what growth areas are you concerned? What hinders growth in those areas? What might be a first step to move forward? What friend could support you as you take new steps toward maturity?

notes

Chapter Three
1. Jesse Nirenberg, *Getting Through to People* (Englewood Cliffs, N.J.: Prentice-Hall, 1963), p. 16.

Chapter Four
1. John Drakeford, *The Awesome Power of the Listening Ear* (Waco, Tex.: Word Books, 1967), p. 26.
2. Robert S. Cathcart and Larry A. Samovar, *Small Group Communication* (Dubuque, Iowa: Wm. C. Brown Co., 1970), p. 257.

Chapter Five
1. Sherod Miller, Elam W. Nunnally, and Daniel B. Wackman, *Alive and Aware* (Minneapolis: Interpersonal Communication Programs, Inc., 1975), p. 109.

Chapter Seven
1. David W. Johnson, *Reaching Out* (Englewood Cliffs, N.J.: Prentice-Hall, 1972), p. 104.
2. Ibid., p. 103.
3. Elizabeth Skoglund, *You Can Be Your Own Child's Counselor* (Glendale, Calif.: G/L Publications, Regal Books, 1978), pp. 54–55.
4. Virginia Satir, *Conjoint Family Therapy* (Palo Alto, Calif.: Science and Behavior Books, 1967), p. 82.

Chapter Eight
1. Nirenberg, *Getting Through,* p. 111.
2. Ibid., p. 42.

Chapter Nine
1. A. W. Tozer, *The Pursuit of God* (Harrisburg, Pa.: Christian Publications, 1948), p. 82.
2. Ibid., p. 74.
3. Ibid., p. 83.
4. Robert A. Williams, *A Place to Belong* (Grand Rapids, Mich.: Zondervan Publishing House, 1972), p. 150.